Th

Chartered psy...
illustrator Ni...

to create a playful and uplifting g...
to positive thinking. Sam has spent many
years helping people take positive action
in their lives by making self-help strategies
engaging, practical and easy to use.

Read the psychologist's top tips and
integrate them into your happier life.

Enjoy the journey!

To: Giselle

With positive thoughts from:

Donna Marks

Get A Grip

Unhappiness often results from attaching importance to events beyond your control. Most of the time you cannot directly control what happens around you, but you can control your reaction to it.

Recognise what is within your control, and keep your focus firmly fixed on that. Categorise everything that you can change in the various areas of your life, for example, personal, professional and health.

Explore

Life should be about the exploration of what is possible. As long it is safe, variety, change and experimentation will broaden your map of the world.

It is through this process that you will learn more about yourself and become better equipped to capture happiness.

The American author and political activist Helen Keller said, "Life is either a daring adventure or nothing... Avoiding danger is no safer in the long-run than exposure."

Widescreen
And High Fidelity

The pictures and sounds that we make in our mind can be made bigger or smaller. When you catch yourself focusing on positive pictures in your mind, make their colour clear and vibrant and enlarge them so that they fill the space in your mind. Do the same to any positive internal sounds by imagining a loudspeaker amplifying them.

A good time to do this is before you go to sleep. Allow your mind to indulge in your happy visions and contentment and well-being will follow.

Smart Symbols

Reminding yourself of the things you love most about life is a sure-fire way to feel happy.

Surround yourself with inspirational quotes, photos of loved ones and certificates of achievement to remind you of your passions. Consider putting images on smartphones and computers, as well as keeping sentimental objects next to your bed. Ideally you should place them in the areas where you spend most of your time. Shaping your environment to work as a force of positive thinking will help you to make happiness a habit.

Be A Dreamer

Living life adventurously and without the fear of failure is beneficial. Get your imagination working on all the possibilities life has to offer by asking yourself the following questions: "What would I do if I knew I couldn't fail?" and, "Who am I when I am at my best?" All great actions start in the mind! Albert Einstein and Walt Disney paid testament to the importance of imagination and indulgent creativity in their great achievements.

Positive Language

How you communicate with others can have an impact on your day-to-day well-being.

Get into the habit of using positive language that avoids focusing on the negative.

For example if you are worried about money, focus your discussions on "getting more money" as opposed to "getting out of debt".
If you concentrate on the latter you will attract even more debt to worry about!

The Super Sunrise

Waking up early every day will boost happiness. Strengthening your connection with nature keeps sadness at bay.
By watching the sunrise and being mindful of your physical senses for several minutes every morning you will be encouraged to ground yourself and feel at peace with your surroundings.

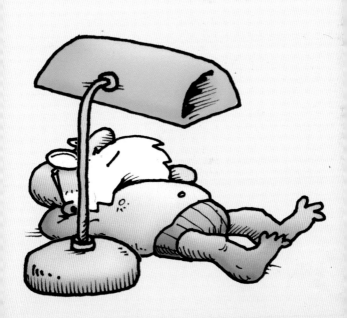

Keep It Simple

Leading a simple life is advisable
in achieving happiness.

Try to cut out the non-essentials
from your life and surround yourself
with objects that will support
your welfare and well-being.
It will help you to become
more self-sufficient and
more aware that happiness
is a choice and not dependent
on what you possess.

Having more can often mean
that you have more to worry about.

The Grass Is
Always Greener

Unhappiness can be created by making unnecessary comparisons with others.

When you feel that you fall short compared to others, low feelings of self-worth and a lack of self-esteem will follow.

Constantly outperforming others is a tiring process and in the long run, not sustainable.

To gain more control over your happiness, focus only on your own personal development.

Let It Go!

When you experience stress and discomfort, it is often difficult to see past the immediate sadness.

Imagine that your focus is a flowing stream and the negative event is a stick on this river.

See and acknowledge it, and then watch it flow out of sight and out of mind down the river. This technique is used within the practice of Zen Buddhism and it will help to prevent you from getting entangled in the negative event.

Gratitude

Giving thanks for what we have is an important process in the pursuit of happiness. You get more of what you focus on, and by exercising gratitude regularly you will train your mind to concentrate on the positives, irrespective of how much or little you may have.

Every day give thanks for as many daily actions and activities as you engage in and life will become more nourishing. Being around loved ones, eating good food and engaging in physical activity are ideal opportunities to practise gratitude.

The Pioneer

Personal development and growth is often dependent on how often we push outside the comfort zone.

The famous German writer Goethe illustrated this point when he said, "Whatever you can do or dream you can, begin it. Boldness has genius, power and magic in it." In your personal and professional life, push your boundaries and challenge yourself. Set the goal of doing one difficult thing each day to continue extending your limits.

It will give you more freedom and ultimately make the goal of happiness easier to achieve.

Bold Bodies

How we feel day-to-day is influenced by how we carry our body. Therefore encourage happy thinking by maintaining a positive posture. Hold your head high, relax your shoulders, keep your back straight and ensure that your breathing is well controlled throughout the day.

Also maintain a comfortable smile to boost your good feelings.

Find A Happy Place

Happiness is like a skill that requires practice in order to work effortlessly. Disciplining and training the mind is the only way to make happiness a habit. Be aware of your thoughts and every time you catch yourself moving towards the negative, break the cycle by immediately refocusing your attention back to the positive. Devise a single yet powerful happy thought and return to this whenever you are distracted by negative thinking. Thinking about the important people in your life provides good material for generating a positive place to concentrate on during testing times.

Beat Boredom

When you feel bored and uninspired, you invite the opportunity to think negatively.

Keep your mind on activities that contribute to your well-being to prevent you feeling discontented and restless. When you feel bored reflect on past achievements and positive memories to prevent your focus from drifting down a negative path. Experiment by changing routines and adding variety to your daily routines.

Take Action

Indecision can create unhappiness. In a world full of possibilities, it is too easy to let opportunities pass by not taking action.

Fear of failure can also limit our desire to seize the moment.

As the former president of the United States, Theodore Roosevelt said, "In a moment of decision the best thing you can do is the right thing. The worst thing you can do is nothing."

The Best Medicine

Learning to laugh more is a sure-fire method to give your sense of well-being a boost.

Watching, reading, listening to comedy and deliberately spending more time with individuals who make you laugh will help you achieve happiness.

Seek out comedians and writers that appeal and explore what the internet has to offer that will make you laugh.

Flourish

Your behaviour should be guided
by your personal values.
A strong connection with
your values and what is
important to you in life
is the most important source of
happiness and contentment.

The Greek philosopher, Aristotle
talked about the importance
of following a set of virtues
in order to flourish and lead
a happy life. Make a list of your
life values as a blueprint for
building happiness.

Story Therapy

Unhappiness often arises when others upset us.

Colleagues, friends, family and even strangers can make us feel negative. When someone behaves badly to you, write it down and turn it into a story.

This technique works in two ways; firstly it helps you to detach and objectify the situation and secondly, by getting creative with the incident you will prevent yourself from dwelling on the negative.

A Happy Ending

The brain is more likely to
remember information
presented to it first and last,
so get into the habit of starting
and ending your daily tasks
on a positive note.

When you reflect on events
at the end of the day,
your memories will be happier
and it will become easier
for the brain to concentrate
on happy states.

The Pocket Psychologist™
Other Titles in the Series

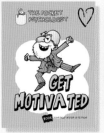

Published by Mindsport Ltd in 2012 - All rights reserved.
Printed in China

Mindsport Ltd
72 Prince Street, Bristol, BS1 4QD, United Kingdom
www.MyPositiveUniverse.com